Peter and the Wolf

Peter and the Wolf

BY VLADIMIR VAGIN

FROM THE SYMPHONY BY SERGEI PROKOFIEV

SCHOLASTIC PRESS ⟷ NEW YORK

*O*nce upon a time, a boy named Peter lived with his grandfather in a little cottage by a meadow and a forest.

One morning, the morning of our story, Grandpapa said to Peter, "A big, hungry wolf has been seen in the forest. You must remember to keep the garden gate shut. And don't play in the meadow. The wolf could come out and eat you!"

Peter listened to his grandfather and did as he was told — most of the time. But this morning, a little bird sat on a branch of a big tree out in the meadow, chirping happily. Peter stopped to listen. He thought, *It's much too nice a day to worry about a wolf.* So, the better to hear the bird's song, Peter opened the gate and went out into the meadow

A duck came waddling through the gate. Peter had left the garden gate
open, you see. The duck waddled over to the lovely pond near the tree.
The little bird and the duck were friends, but the bird felt the pond and
the meadow belonged to her, and she flew over to pester the duck.

"What kind of bird are you," the little bird chirped, "when you don't
even fly?"

"And what kind of bird are you," quacked the duck, "when you can't
even swim?"

And so they argued, the duck splashing and diving in the
water, and the little bird fluttering and hopping
along the edge of the pond.

Suddenly, something caught Peter's eye. Was it the wolf? No, it was just the farmyard cat, slowly crawling through the grass toward the pond.

The cat thought, *I'll just grab that little bird before he even notices I'm here*. Closer and closer, closer and closer she crept.

Peter saw what the cat was up to.

"Look out, little bird!" he shouted.

The bird flew up into the tree to safety.

The duck quacked angrily at the cat from the middle of the pond. "Leave my friend alone!" he cried.

But the cat was not interested in the duck. She crawled around and around the tree and considered again how to catch the bird. *If I climb up the tree,* she thought, *will he only fly away?*

Just then, Grandpapa came out. He saw Peter in the meadow, and saw that he had left the gate open too, and he was angry.

"What would you do if the wolf came out?" Grandpapa scolded as he marched Peter home. But Peter did not listen. He was not the sort of boy to be afraid of a wolf.

No sooner had Peter and Grandpapa gone inside the gate, and Grandpapa gone into the cottage, than the big gray wolf came out of the forest. He crept toward the pond, staying well-hidden.

Just then, the cat scampered up the tree after the bird.

"Look out!" quacked the duck to the bird. In his excitement, he jumped

out of the pond — and right in front of the wolf!

The duck ran as fast as he could. But the wolf got closer . . .
and closer . . .

and closer . . . until, with one gulp, he swallowed the duck whole.

Then the wolf began to pace around and around the tree, greedily eyeing the cat. Meanwhile, the cat crept down the branch toward the little bird. Peter saw all that was going on from behind the closed gate. All at once, he knew just how to rescue his friends and catch the wolf. But he must be quick!

Peter ran and found a strong rope. Then he climbed onto the high stone wall, so that he was in reach of a branch of the tree. To catch the wolf, Peter would need the little bird's help.

First, he climbed onto the tree and scared the cat away. Then, he whispered to the bird, "Fly down around the wolf's head. But be careful he doesn't catch you!"

The bird flew off the branch and fluttered all around the wolf's head, brushing his nose with her wings and making him very angry. Just when the wolf thought he had caught the bird, she would dash away.

Peter inched out on the branch till he was right over the wolf. He made a lasso with the rope and lowered it down. Deftly he looped the lasso around the wolf's tail, and with a mighty pull, he cinched the rope tight.

Peter had caught the wolf!

The wolf struggled hard to get away. But the more he jumped, the more the rope tightened around his tail. Peter tied the other end of the rope to the tree and called down, "I'm not afraid of some old wolf!"

Just then, a group of hunters came crashing and stomping out of the forest, pointing their guns all around and looking for the wolf.

"Don't shoot!" Peter shouted to them. "Look here! The bird and I have already caught the wolf!"

"The wolf is very dangerous!" called the hunters. "Hand him over to us."

"No," said Peter. "You mustn't hurt him. Help us take him to the zoo!"

What a procession they made!

Peter led the way, of course. Then came the hunters, leading the wolf with the rope. Then came Grandpapa and the cat. Grandpapa could hardly contain his pride, though he had been angry earlier.

"He's a brave boy, my Peter," Grandpapa said.

Above them all flew the little bird, chirping merrily, "Look what we have caught, Peter and I!"

And what about the duck?

All the way to the zoo, he sat quacking inside the wolf, perfectly whole and well. He made such a noise that the wolf spat him out, and he returned with Peter to quack many another day.

About the Music

Vladimir Vagin's retelling of *Peter and the Wolf* is adapted from a symphony by Russian composer, Sergei Prokofiev. Prokofiev loved telling stories with his music, and in this symphony he set out to compose a piece of music for young people that would both thrill them with a story and introduce the sounds of an orchestra. Here, the musical themes, each played by a different musical instrument, represent different characters. (All music examples are written at concert pitch.)

Peter has the jaunty and confident notes of the *violin*

Grandfather has the deep and strong notes of the *bassoon*

Duck has the short and determined notes of the *oboe*

Cat has the slinky and swift notes of the *clarinet*

Wolf has the ominous and sure notes of the *French horns*

The *Hunters* have the sudden and booming notes of the *kettle drum*

Bird has the jumpy and sweet notes of the *flute*

About the Composer

Sergei Prokofiev was born in 1891 in Sontzovka, Ukraine. His formal music career began when he entered the St. Petersburg Conservatory at the age of thirteen as a pianist, though he had already started to compose music on his own. After graduating with honors, Prokofiev went on to travel, going to England first, then the United States. There he composed perhaps his most important and distinct pieces from his early career, "The Classical Symphony" (1917), which blended "classical" eighteenth century rhythms with modern harmonies.

In 1922, Prokofiev moved to France. He took on more and more commissions from the Soviet Union while in France, and eventually moved back to his homeland in 1936. Prokofiev encountered enormous limitations and censorship in the Soviet Union from Stalin's government, however, and many of his works were banned. Yet, some of the pieces composed during the time he was in France and his later years in the Soviet Union are among the most lyrical and well-known of his compositions. They include, "Lieutenant Kije" (1933), "Romeo and Juliet" (1936), and "Peter and the Wolf" (1936).

During his entire career, Sergei Prokofiev composed 6 operas, 6 ballets, 7 symphonies, about 12 orchestral works, 5 piano concertos, 2 violin concertos, and many other works of chamber music, piano pieces, songs, and choral pieces. He died in 1953 in Moscow, Russia. Prokofiev remains one of the most important composers of the twentieth century.

~ to Anna Kolesnitchenko ~

Copyright © 2000 by Vladimir Vagin ▪ All rights reserved. ▪ Published by Scholastic Press, a division of Scholastic Inc., *Publishers since 1920.* SCHOLASTIC, SCHOLASTIC PRESS, and associated logos are trademarks and/or registered trademarks of Scholastic Inc. ▪ No part of this publication may be reproduced, or stored in a retrieval system, or transmitted in any form or by any means, electronic, mechanical, photocopying, recording, or otherwise, without written permission of the publisher. For information regarding permission, write to Scholastic Inc., Attention: Permissions Department, 555 Broadway, New York, NY 10012 ▪ LIBRARY OF CONGRESS CATALOGING-IN-PUBLICATION DATA ▪ Vagin, Vladimir / Peter and the wolf / by Vladimir Vagin p. cm. ▪ "From the story of a symphony by Sergei Prokofiev." Summary: Retells the orchestral fairy tale of the boy who, ignoring his grandfather's warning, proceeds to capture a wolf with the help of his friend the bird. ▪ ISBN 0-590-38608-5 ▪ [1. Fairy tales.] I. Prokofiev, Sergei, 1891–1953. Peëiv i volk. II. Title PZ8.V15 Pe2000 [E]—dc21 99-047590 ▪ CIP ▪ Book design by Marijka Kostiw ▪ The art for this book was created using pencil and watercolors. The text was set in Galliard 15/25. ▪ The display type was set in Byron Bold. ▪ 10 9 8 7 6 5 4 3 2 1   0/0 01 02 03 04 ▪ Printed in Singapore 46 ▪ First Edition, November 2000